Build-a-Skill Instant Books
Sight Words, Part 2

Written by
Rozanne Lanczak Williams

Editor: Stacey Faulkner
Illustrator: Darcy Tom
Cover Illustrator: Rick Grayson
Designer: The Development Source
Art Director: Moonhee Pak
Project Director: Betsy Morris

© 2007 Creative Teaching Press Inc., Huntington Beach, CA 92649
Reproduction of activities in any manner for use in the classroom and not for commercial sale is permissible.
Reproduction of these materials for an entire school or for a school system is strictly prohibited.

Table of Contents

Introduction 2
Making and Using the Instant Books 3

Instant Books

Flip Books 5
Mini Flip Book 6
Read-and-Write Book 7
Sight Word Cards 8
Make Your Own Word Cards 14
Strip Book (an, day) 15
Strip Book (very, long, day) 16
Mini Book (know, about) 17
Strip Book (called, said) 18
Flip Book
   (many, people, live, him, her, them, us) ... 19
Mini Book (then, some) 20
Strip Book (jump, out, of, into) 21
Strip Book (who, lives) 22
Flip Book (take, two, many, some, more) ... 23
Fold-a-Book (which) 24
Flip Book (which, our, their, his, her) 25
Mini Book (time, just) 26
Flip Book (would, could, did, eat) 27
Fold-a-Book (if, could, where, would) 28
Strip Book (over, said, down) 29
Fold-a-Book (when, was, now, little, but) 30
Mini Book
   (very, good, but, only, eat, little) 31
Strip Book (ever, been, would, again, yes) .. 32

Introduction

About the Build-a-Skill Instant Books Series

The *Build-a-Skill Instant Books* series features a variety of reproducible instant books that focus on important reading and math skills covered in the primary classroom. Each instant book is easy to make, and once children become familiar with the basic formats that appear throughout the series, they will be able to make new books with little help. Children will love the unique, manipulative quality of the books and will want to read them over and over again as they gain mastery of basic learning skills!

About the Build-a-Skill Instant Books: Sight Words, Part 2

This book features 50 sight words in fun and easy-to-make instant books. Children will develop fine motor skills and practice following directions as they cut, fold, and staple the reproducible pages together to make flip books, strip books, mini books, and more! As children read and reread their instant books, they will increase their immediate recognition of sight word vocabulary, and they will build fluency and comprehension skills.

Refer to the Table of Contents to help with lesson planning. Choose instant book activities that fit with the curriculum goals in your regular or ELL classroom. Use the instant books to practice skills or introduce new ones. Directions for making the instant books appear on pages 3 and 4. These should be copied and sent along with the book patterns when assigning a bookmaking activity as homework.

Making and Using the Instant Books

All of the instant books in this resource require only one or two pieces of paper. Copy the pages on white copy paper or card stock, or use colored paper to jazz up and vary the formats. Children will love personalizing their instant books by coloring them, adding construction paper covers, or decorating them with collage materials such as wiggly eyes, ribbon, and stickers. Customize the instant books by adding extra pages, or by creating your own word cards using the reproducible on page 14.

Children can make instant books as an enrichment activity when their regular classwork is done, as a learning center activity during guided reading time, or as a homework assignment. They can place completed instant books in their classroom book boxes and then read and reread the books independently or with a reading buddy. After children have had many opportunities to read their books in school, send the books home for extra skill-building practice. Encourage children to store the books in a special box that they have labeled "I Can Read Box."

Directions for Making the Instant Books

There are seven basic formats for the instant books in this guide. The directions appear below for quick and easy reference. The directions are written *to* the child, in case you would like to send the bookmaking activities home as homework. Just copy the directions and attach them to the instant book pages.

Hint! To have children practice reading sight words in isolation use the word cards on pages 8–13 with any of the instant books on pages 5–7. As a rule of thumb, six to ten cards can be easily stapled onto each booklet. To have children practice reading sight words in context, use the instant books on pages 15–32.

Flip Books, page 5

1. Cut out the two flip books, word cards, and blank word cards.
2. Staple the word cards to the "I can read" flip book.
3. Staple the blank word cards to the "I can write" flip book.
4. "Flip up" each card to practice reading and writing your sight words.

Mini Flip Book (makes 2), page 6

1. Cut out the mini flip book and word cards.
2. Staple the word cards to the mini flip book.
3. Practice reading your sight words.

Read-and-Write Book, page 7

1. Cut out the read-and-write book.
2. Glue the book to a piece of construction paper the same size.
3. Cut out the word cards. Staple the cards to the top strip.
4. Fold the book in half and decorate the cover.
5. Practice reading and writing your sight words.

Strip Book, pages 15, 16, 18, 21, 22, 29, 32

1. Finish the book by tracing and/or writing the words.
2. Cut out the strips.
3. Put the pages in order. Staple them on the left.

Optional: Make and decorate a construction paper cover, and color the pictures.

Mini Book, pages 17, 20, 26, 31

1. Finish the book by tracing and/or writing the words.
2. Draw any missing pictures.
3. Cut along the solid lines to make four pages.
4. Put the pages in order. Staple them on the left.

Optional: Make and decorate a construction paper cover, and color the pictures.

Flip Book, pages 19, 23, 25, 27

1. Trace the dotted words.
2. Cut out the flip book and the four word cards.
3. Staple the word cards to the flip book.
4. "Flip up" each card to practice reading your sight words.

Fold-a-Book, pages 24, 28, 30

1. Finish the book by tracing and/or writing the words.
2. Draw any missing pictures.
3. Cut along the outside solid lines. Fold the book on the dotted lines.

Optional: Make and decorate a construction paper cover, and color the pictures.

Flip Books

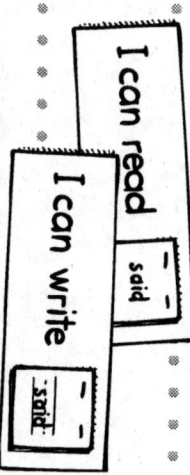

I can read

Staple word cards here.

I can write

Staple word cards here.

Mini Flip Book

____'s
Word Book

Staple word cards here.

____'s
Word Book

Staple word cards here.

Read-and-Write Book

I can read

I can write

Staple word cards here.

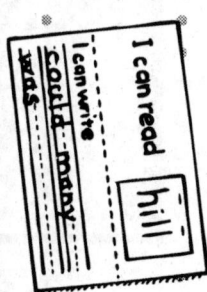

Sight Word Cards

an	day	very
long	know	about
called	said	many

Sight Word Cards

people	live	him
her	them	us
then	some	jump

Sight Word Cards

out	of	into
who	take	two
more	when	_____

Sight Word Cards

was	now	little
but	time	just
would	could	_____

Sight Word Cards

did	ever	eat
if	where	over
down	which	_____

Sight Word Cards

our	their	his
good	only	been
again	yes	___

Make Your Own Word Cards

an, day — Strip Book

An apple a day,
an apple a day,

1

an apple a day,
keeps the doctor away!

2

An orange a day,
an orange a day,

3

___ orange a ___,
keeps the doctor away!

4

very, long, day Strip Book

The Very Long Day

I had a very long bus ride.

I had a very long walk.

I had a very long lunch.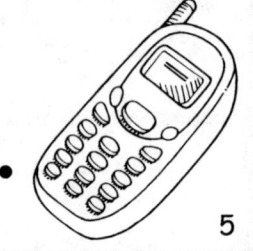

I had a very long talk.

I had a _____ _____ day!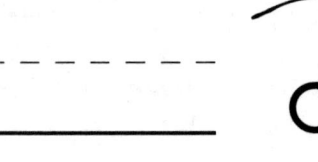

know, about | Mini Book

What I Know

by _____

I know about art.

I know about math.

I _____ science.

I know I am smart!

called, said — Strip Book

Miss Lucy called the doctor.
Miss Lucy called the nurse.

Miss Lucy called the lady with the alligator purse.

"Soup!" said the doctor.
"Popcorn!" said the nurse.

"Pizza!" _____ the lady with the alligator purse.

many, people, live, him, her, them, us

Flip Book

Staple word cards here.

Many people live by me.

him

her

them

us

then, some

Mini Book

My Mud Pies

First I get some dirt.

1

Then I get some water.

2

Then I get some spoons.

3

_____ I mix it up!

4

jump, out, of, into *Strip Book*

Jump into the pool.

Jump out of the sand.

Jump into the leaves.

Jump out of the mud.

_____ into the tub!

who, lives Strip Book

Who lives in the desert?
Who lives in a tree?

1

Who lives in a pond?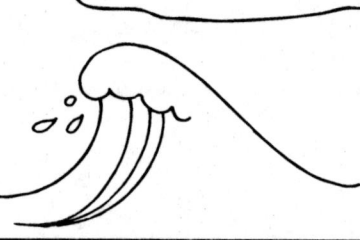
Who lives in the sea?

2

A snake lives in the desert.
An owl lives in a tree.

3

A frog _____ in a pond.
A whale _____ in the sea.

4

22

take, two, many, some, more

Flip Book

I can take

three

apples.

Staple word cards here.

two

many

some

more

which Fold-a-Book

(page 3, upside down) Which pet do you like?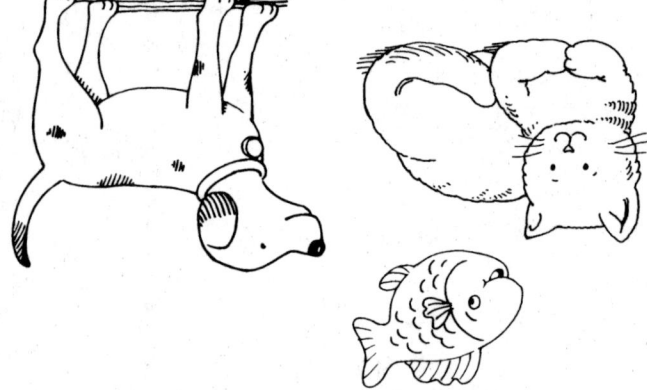

(page 2, upside down) Which color do you like?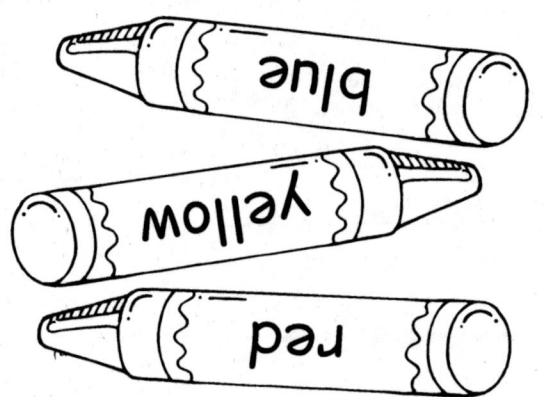

Which ice cream do you like?

_____

Which One Do You Like?

by _____

which, our, their, his, her

Flip Book

Which one is your house?

Staple word cards here.

their

his

her

our

time, just
Mini Book

Time to Play

It is just one o'clock.
I have lots of
time to play.

1

It is just
three o'clock.
I have lots
of time to play.

2

It is just
seven o'clock.
I have lots
of time to play.

3

It is _____
nine o'clock.
I have no more
_____ to play!

4

would, could, will, did, eat

Flip Book

if, could, where, would — Fold-a-Book

3

If a pig could fly, where would it fly?

2

If a cat could fly, where would it fly?

If . . .

If a dog could fly, where would it fly?

1

If you _____ fly, where _____ you fly?

4

over, said, down — Strip Book

"Come over," said Mr. Wolf.
"Sit down on the chair."

"Come over," said Mr. Wolf.
"Sit down on the grass."

"Come ____," ____ Mr. Wolf.
"Sit ____ in the pot."

"No thank you, Mr. Wolf!"

when, was, now, little, but — Fold-a-Book

3

When I was little, I had a crib.

2

But now, I have a cup.

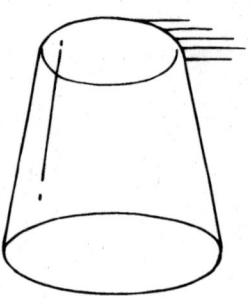

But now, I have a bed.

4

When I Was Little

When I was little, I had a bottle.

1

very, good, but, only, eat, little | Mini Book

Very Good!

This soup is very good,
but I can only eat a little.

1

This fruit is very good,
but I can only eat a little.

3

This bread is very good,
but I can only eat a little.

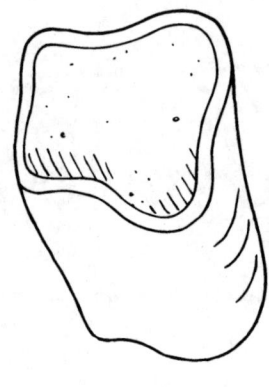

2

This _____ is very good.
I can eat it all! Yum!

4

ever, been, would, again, yes — Strip Book

Have You Ever Been There?

Have you ever been to the zoo?
Would you ever go again?

Have you ever been to the farm?
Would you ever go again?

Have you ever been to the circus?
Would you ever go again?

Have you ever been to the _____?
Yes, yes, yes! I would go again!